Ben Anderson / Matthew Kelly / Katrina Navickas / Ian Waites

Decommissioning the twentieth century

Uniformbooks

Uniformbooks
7 Hillhead Terrace, Axminster, Devon EX13 5JL
uniformbooks.co.uk

Trade distribution in the UK by Central Books
centralbooks.com

Printed and bound by Pureprint, Uckfield, Sussex

Ben Anderson

Rural Modernism

1. Kristen Bluemel and Michael McCluskey (eds.),
   Rural Modernity in Britain: A Critical Intervention
   (Edinburgh: Edinburgh University Press, 2018).
2. John Sheail, 'Pesticides and the British
   Environment: An Agricultural Perspective',
   Environment and History 19:1 (2013), pp.87–108.
3. Matthew Kelly 'Conventional Thinking and the
   Fragile Birth of the Nature State in Post-War
   Britain', in Wilko Graf von Hardenberg, et al
   (eds.), *The Nature State: Rethinking the History
   of Conservation* (Abingdon: Routledge, 2017),
   pp.114–134.
4. Natalie Zemon Davis, 'On the Lame', *American
   Historical Review* 93:3 (1988), pp.572–603;
   Essays in Robert Perks (ed.), *The Oral History
   Reader* (Abingdon: Routledge, 2016), Part III,
   pp.297–444; Steven High, *Corporate Wasteland:
   The Landscape and Memory of Deindustrialization*
   (Ithaca: Cornell University Press, 2007), pp.13–
   18, pp.58–62.
5. See *chatterleywhitfield.online*.

As a small Derbyshire child, on the way back home from a visit to grandparents in the South, I waited for a belt of cooling towers and chimneys that marked, for me, the North. They still surround a short section of the M1, as it travels between Derby and Nottingham, standing like sentries over the Trent Valley, and the advent of hillier, more exciting country after the endless flat fields of junctions one to twenty-four. Nor was I alone. As we found out while researching the demise of these structures and the landscapes they so altered, this experience was common, quintessential even, for the British population as it travelled on the motorways constructed alongside the power stations. Irrespective of aesthetic judgement or other personal connection, for Northerners northbound the vast curved concrete towers of the Trent's 'megawatt valley' meant 'home'. A response of this sort was not limited to power stations or Megawatt Valley, as important as they were. The vast carbon infrastructure of the Twentieth Century, from oil-refineries to power stations, from mining tips or collieries, defined how people encountered the landscapes of Britain for fifty years, providing landmarks for navigating a new world of electricity, rapid travel, and consumerism.

The changes of the post-war era were of course more profound, as lives everywhere were touched by new technologies, politics and demographies, but this new imaginary map of the country points to just how far those changes were about a *rural* modernisation even for the increasingly urban population. The great symbolic technological systems of the era were rural in imagination and infrastructure: the pylons and power stations of the national grid, the bitumen curves of motorways, or the masts of the new national television network.[1] Equally, rural residents—and especially farmers—were marshalled by governments committed to improving food security through new, more efficient, and often more environmentally-lethal agricultural practices.[2] Where once the absence of National Parks made Britain an international outlier, now vast areas of the countryside would, in theory at least, be set aside as places for a nation to enjoy the outdoors.[3] Before the Second World War, it might have credibly been claimed that Britain's rural areas remained steadfastly 'unmodern',

now they would be dragged into the new age by the state—
whether they liked it or not.

Even as it was being built, this new modernity fell short
of the utopian visions that compelled its development, and
relied on a fragile and short-lived 'post-war consensus'.
By the mid-twentieth century, globalisation, and political
choices about Britain's economic future had already radically
altered the landscapes of the North, Scotland and Wales, and
the myriad social, economic and cultural consequences of
deindustrialisation are still with us. In the early decades of the
twenty-first, much of the remaining infrastructure of post-war
development is disappearing too, in search of a solution to
the climate change it helped create. The demolition of cooling
towers has become a regular feature in online news feeds,
even if the loss felt by nearby communities and workers who
rightfully took pride in hosting these facilities does not. The
sites discussed here—two decommissioned power stations, a
long-standing coal heritage site, and a gritstone edge—are a
part of the varied stories of rural transformation in the late-
twentieth century. Two—Fawley Power Station on the west
bank of Southampton Water as it drains into the Solent, and
West Burton Power Station, near Gainsborough in the lower-
Trent Valley—were once hyper-modern symbols of fossil-fuel
modernity, and aesthetically celebrated as landmarks of
efficiency and clean power. Both recently decommissioned,
their futures remain dictated by their past. West Burton's
rural position, size and iconic design will now host a fusion-
generation experiment, and continue its story of rural
modernism. Fawley's future, meanwhile, looks like a different
form of modernity altogether—here, a new town is slated to
emerge on the banks of Southampton Water.

Elsewhere, we visit sites of rural modernity which blend an
older history of innovation and newness with the impacts of
the post-war focus on the new and the countryside. Blackstone
Edge, a short outcropping of gritstone overlooking Rochdale
and Manchester, distils not just the austerities of Northern
moorland but also has been made subject to whatever 'modern'
meant at any particular time. It is a landscape at once bleak
and uncompromising, yet also cut with the incisions of

human need. The pylons and nearby M62 might seem to sit uncomfortably with the pack-horse 'roman' road, drainage ditches and radical politics, but they are of a piece in this constantly threatened and exploited, but loved and well-trodden land. The cultural significance of the 'post-industrial' rural landscape, so often viewed solely as sites of extraction, is also taken up in a foray into one of Britain's largest and most complete deep-mine collieries. The history of the rural modern goes underland here, as miners adapted and struggled with an ever-changing landscape both above and below. Yet the mine's spaces—both before and after closure—deserve as much attention as those on Blackstone Edge, each claiming their place in the history of Rural Modernity.

How do historians imagine the past?

When I sit down in an archive, or talk to people at a conference, or sit down to write, I'm never just regurgitating evidence to form an argument. Instead, the evidence paints a world in my head, which I then try to describe as best I can. Unless it is made an explicit part of a text, this imaginative part of history work is rarely discussed. Indeed, when that does happen, it often becomes a point of controversy: think of those microhistories criticised for supposed embellishment of source material, or of personal narratives that organise time and place in 'inaccurate' ways, or of the personal writing of a site that buries dynamics of exploitation and struggle.[4] These debates about the limits that can or should be placed on historical knowledge are necessary and useful, but they have also fetishized histories in which the imagination of the past is most visible, as if to deny its presence in all historical research.

All the contributors to the volume have been researchers alongside artists on an Arts and Humanities Research Council-funded project called 'Decommissioning the Twentieth Century', which sought to utilise socially-engaged art as a research method.[5] The process required us, as historians, to take a step back from our work and approach it from a new position in which we abandoned any sharp distinction between imaginative work on the heritage of our sites, and evidence-based objective records of the past. The project invited participants to engage creatively in the memory, pasts and heritages of sites as they were decommissioned, and that went for us too—we wanted to know what would happen if we decommissioned certain of our professional restraints and foregrounded the imaginative and experiential part of writing history.

The book starts from the premise that a creative imagination is central to all history writing, and these pieces should be interpreted as our own encounters with these spaces and their potential, rather than as historical account circumscribed by the limits of the documentary evidence. To write about an event, to explain its sequence and the behaviours of its protagonists and antagonists, means to empathise with countless people as they went about their lives. This happens inevitably, because the worlds that often seem to be right there in our sources we imagine into being, almost unwittingly drawn into our wider knowledge of period and place. We might sometimes will these past worlds into being by going to the place itself, or to the place at it is now, hoping this will allow us to access all those fugitive intangibles that escaped the documentary evidence, or we seek out the ways in which a time and place was imagined in its film, music, literature, and images. The following four short texts all aim to foreground that exercise—they are (possibly foolhardy) attempts by historians to reveal the creativity of historical thought before we engage our empirical other selves and expunge the worlds we have created from our heads.

Ben Anderson

Chatterley Whitfield

Photographs

1. Clothes hanging underground near a storage area, late-twentieth century.
2. Chatterley Whitfield Pithead Baths and Catering Block, early 1990s.
3. Interior view looking along the disused colliery's locker room.
4. Hesketh Headgear and Tub Hall, 1975.
5. The Winstanley Underground Tour at Chatterley Whitfield, mid-1980s.
6. Chatterley Whitfield Mining Museum poster, early-1990s.
7. Art Deco Office block, Chatterley Whitfield, 2022.
8. The Bowling Alley Seam.
9. Private notice sign in front of Chatterley Whitfield tip, May 1965.
10. View of Chatterley Whitfield from the Tip, mid-1950s.
11. Barn Owl at Chatterley Whitfield, August 2022

These reflections are meant to be about spaces, as people used them (in my own imagination at least), and the meanings that use might have created. It's a set of topics that historians rarely get to answer with this level of license. So, no claims to accuracy then, but the following is based on research in the archive held by the Chatterley Whitfield Friends at the colliery: documents, histories, and testimony from now-deceased miners. Many thanks to the Friends, and especially to Lloyd Boardman, who read the pieces for accuracy and sensitivity. I hope they do the colliery justice.

Miners' showers and catering block, 1938

As I run my fingers over the past, there is a sound I wasn't expecting: hymns. Not just one person, but hundreds, standing naked in little pools of blackened water, over two floors, as their collective voice competes with the metal-on-metal and air-on-air of the colliery. Out there and underground, the machines drown the miners, but in here, the rush of the showers is inaudible over hymn after hymn after hymn.

They're in good voice. The songs are drawn from the churches and chapels in the heartland of Wesleyan methodism, and led by choir members whose voices drowned out the more dubious contributions. The singing seems appropriate too, because in these spaces, miners enter and exit the underground; an in-between daily ritual, albeit one that separates public and private, work and leisure; a cleansing for a return to citizenship after the sacrifice of the mine.

Perhaps it is for this reason that guards in small booths watch entry so carefully: amongst the bright green tiles, clean citizens, and dirty miners each have their own lockers and rooms. There are limits too, on behaviour under the water. The

3

curtains initially provided to soothe the architect's prudishness are long gone, some pulled down through accident, or to hold water so as to continue the games and tricks of underground friendship. Those used to a life of hot, semi-naked work underground are hardly likely to be concerned at sight of the same bodies above. Other pranks abound. Men arriving from the pit need a full-body scrub to clear the dust from their skin; so they scrub each other's backs, revealing from under each layer of grey and black a greater variety of skin-tones, drawn from across Britain, Europe and a moribund Empire. In one cubicle, a miner squeals when a bucket of cold water appears from nowhere, others control a smile as a giant leaves with a forehead still black with dust, while another searches frantically for a towel that has gone missing. So far, so harmless—but there are also odd miners walking home in their dirt, banned for behaviour against the showers too offensive to tolerate. A shower-ban might rarely last more than a couple of weeks, but unlike stints on tough jobs borne with resilience and even pride, or small wage reductions, returning in real dirt means returning in metaphorical dirt too. It means honesty to the family, and wives, mothers and daughters thrown back to a world of tin baths in front of the hearth, often after their own long day at a pottery factory.

The cleansing might only be external, since dust on the inside of lungs can't just be sung away, but it is real, and a feast awaits in the canteen. Its staff were long the only women on the site, and still serve impressively meaty pies, bacon butties, sausages and bottles of milk to clean miners sat in groups, at tables designed by smaller men. They chat and gossip in a rounded bay window of the art-deco shower and canteen block, perhaps putting off one family at home in favour of another at the pit.

When they do go, though, they return home as they came, as the new model citizens advertised by National Coal Board publicity. British Stakhanovites who leave the pit at the pit, and walk without the accompanying clanks of personal kit. The showers date from a different era, to be sure, but it is under them, amongst those hymns, that the miner becomes a part of post-war modernity.

4

18 CHATTERLEY WHITFIELD

Under Winstanley, 1979, in the sidings, 1986

Seven-hundred feet down, passing cables and tiny cages, methane-choked pockets, and flooded shafts and roads, there is a submerged museum. On the walls there are signs, originally for miners but now repurposed for their children and grandchildren. They detail the rules of the underworld "CONTRABAND includes cigarettes, and CONTRIVANCES for SMOKING... LIABLE to PROSECUTION under the MINES and QUARRIES ACT", "Before the person enters the cage, the onsetter shall signal to the banksman and to the winding engineman—3", "no material shall be carried through a shaft whilst persons are being carried through it, whether in the same direction or not".

There isn't much here to suggest a museum at all. There are no interpretative boards or demonstration equipment and few warning signs—little to distinguish this area from any other in the mine. For that, we need to empty the water out, carefully

5

store the methane, unplug the shaft, reinstall the car, and repopulate with the dwindling number of ex-miner guides and experts. Here's the truth of the place: the objects aren't interpreted, because they aren't the exhibits. They are just part of the space, much like the chaotic and frankly worrying roof supports, the narrow-gauge rails or even that mysterious set of cogs in the corner that no-one seems to know the purpose of. The museum is, rather, a stage for the ex-miners, a place for their show, in which the exhibits interpret themselves. The museum is interactive, to be sure, as children and parents ask questions, use picks on real coal faces or knock out supports. This place was about the skill of the mine, and the

Chatterley Whitfield Mining Museum

NEW HOME OF THE BRITISH COAL COLLECTION

TRIPS UNDERGROUND 10.00-4.00; SITE OPEN
10.00-5.00. OPEN 7 DAYS A WEEK
INCLUDING BANK HOLIDAYS
SUPERB SOUVENIR SHOP & CANTEEN!

CHATTERLEY WHITFIELD MINING MUSEUM
STOKE-ON-TRENT. TEL: 0782 813337

modernity of the miner at a time when, three miles away, but in the same complex of seams, beds, shafts and roads, coal was still worth digging for.

The pumps in the Wolstanton 'superpit' kept the under-ground museum at Chatterley Whitfield dry—and open. Wolstanton ceased to draw coal in 1984, it also ceased to pump water, and the museum lost a unique attraction. Yet within three years, this intensely resourceful museum had built a replacement. A whole, fake 'underground' emerged in a rail-way siding, with what was a very convincing descent into the depths and another genuine coal face to work. By the time it opened, however, the industrial context had changed. Coal was no longer in decline; it had gone, even if the nearby pit at Silverdale would struggle on for another decade. Now in the early-1990s, the museum is undeniably heritage—but still, this is a place of a living industry, a place to meet former miners, to explain and demonstrate skill and a connection between an older generation of men, and the schoolchildren who increasingly become their visitors. The children's minds stick on the descent down: a journey of only about ten metres, made to feel like several hundred by using rolling sheets of brickwork, and a bit of acting on the part of the tour guides. There's plenty more exhibited here—and especially now that the space is designed to accommodate it—but somehow, it is still that moment of knowing intergenerational performance that defines a visit.

The Surveyors' Office, 1934

There's a white line on the roof on the ten-foot seam drift, and bits of string hang down from it. The line is meant to be straight, because in a mine where conveyor belts move the coal, drifts must be also be straight, and that's not easy underground, with no landmarks, and little light. The line is never straight though, because it is painted on a moving surface. Each morning, surveyors arrive. They check the strings to record movement, settling earth, bending girders, collapsed holes, chain-reactions from half-forgotten seams packed long ago. Then, they record, check, and repaint the line. At the face, miners find themselves working in a slightly altered direction. This world is all measured relative to the colliery's iconic, 2000ft deep Hesketh shaft, and it all keeps moving.

All that movement produces an endless stream of documentation above ground, in a well-lit room in the top of Chatterley Whitfield's brazenly art-deco office block (shown overleaf). Surveyors and their clerks, bearing miners' clothes, but not their bodies, pass information from the underground, and reproduce it, free of dust and sweat in the world above. For many pits, the detailed plans, diagrams, maps, cross-sections and analyses produced by surveyors and their draftsmen will be all that remain: All the surveyors dig out from the mine are numbers and measurements, drafts and data, but these prove more enduring than the coal. The information is all hauled to the pithead, and over to the clean, bright, and dust-free spaces of the surveyor's office. Here, men working on large tilted boards, alongside cups of tea and with an unlikely precision, prepare diagrams, charts and maps to guide the future of the mine.

These plans, maps and diagrams are incomprehensible outside of mining. Their language is always an attempt to render a radically three-dimensional operation into the two available on paper. There are cross-sections of the pit, vertical descriptions of veins, maps of the surface superimposed with worked-out areas or coal ownership, and of course, attempts to chart the underground complex of shafts, roads and cruts for everything from coal extraction to ventilation. The surveyors are joined by a whole host of other workers whose purpose is to produce technical drawings and schemata. Engineers describe new machinery, scientists produce quality reports from the lab, and geologists note strata and where new seams might lie. Their work is essential in a pit of this size, and make the mine intelligible, or at least to those with the power to direct it.

The need to measure, record and document neverthe-less means facing the pit in all its brutality. Once hope of rescue ceases, surveyors are amongst the first at the scene of accidents; to them falls the grisly, but respectful and clear-ly-venerated task of recording who fell where, and why. The schematic diagrams are disconcerting; produced with clear care and deep responsibility, they describe often explosive accidents in impossibly straight, well-ordered tunnels; the destruction of the disasters is rarely made visible. In each document, crucial for subsequent inquiries and investigations, the emotive content could only be expressed in the care of production, and use of colour, but even so, it is not difficult to detect. Corpses are indicated, too; carefully assigned a position with an X, and, since surveyors cannot provide a cause of death, terse description: 'Pinky' for carbon-monoxide poisoning; burnt, singed, fractured, gassed.

Snapping. Narrow seams. Mid-twentieth century

When surveyors describe a shaft, they produce a vertical column of endless layers of coal, each carrying its own name —Moss, Bellringer, Bowling Alley, Bambury. White, hashed, shaded or coloured for earth, rock or shale, and jet black for coal. Even a cursory glance reveals the complexity of the field, but also—these seams are *thin*.

Not all of them, admittedly. On the tallest faces the coal might run to six feet tall. Many stoop to work the face, but make no mistake: this is easy work by comparison. On the narrow seams—the Brights, Littlerow, or Yard—the miners don't excavate a place to stand; lifting earth from the colliery only costs money. Instead, they work as naked as they dare, in three-foot high roads, on hands, knees, sides and bellies. As compensation, the coal they dig is worth more; a penny per tonne for every inch under three foot of height. Now, they strive to keep the roof low, the extra discomfort judged to be worth the extra pay.

The mine is supported by a vast number of underground specialists—mechanics, electricians, carpenters, packers, etc, but even so, the whole process requires constant ingenuity and invention. Roof supports have to be manufactured to fit, and what they support might well be any old piece of recycled steel plate or wood. The machinery has to be built to work in conditions of dirt and dust, but despite constant oiling, routinely clogs up, and often the mechanics simply strip, clean and reassemble. Each stoppage is decried by overseers and miners alike. In one tunnel, a drive shaft releases sparks: in an environment of flammable gas potentially disastrous. The mechanic moves to shut it down, but the overseer appears, insists on keeping it

running, and simply redirects a nearby spray for keeping dust down onto the shaft.

Miners don't really like to rest, but time to eat their 'snapping'—sandwiches, pies or oatcakes—is still a marked time in each shift. The men sit around, laughing and joking for the twenty minutes, propped up as best they can under a low ceiling and against roof supports. The space is shared too by some of the other residents of the mine—mice, cockroaches and rats. To make sure they keep precious food out of harm's way, the

miners hang it up, alongside shirts, jackets and other clothes
—regularly swapped around when unguarded property is fair
game.

   Jokes and tricks keep the men together: you don't get that
spirit just because you are all from the same village. Indeed,
like many coal mines after the second world war, the sons of
earlier generations of Staffordshire mining families are joined
by workers from North-East England, South Wales, central
Scotland, Eire, Italy, Yugoslavia, Poland, Italy, Ukraine or the

Baltic states—and later and in smaller numbers, from the Caribbean, India or South Africa. Camaraderie based on pranks involving itching powder or fake errand shades into sustained campaigns aimed to instill disliked nicknames on authority figures—an overmanager known as 'hankie' encounters ever-increasing bouts of sneezing wherever he goes. In no small measure, the pit relies on that solidarity—a hidden contribution to safety, mutual understanding, tolerance of mistakes and long hours demanded by the mine that throws these men together. But though almost all miners attest to the comraderie of the pit, the friendships that it creates and sustains do not necessarily break down barriers above ground. So too, these aspects of life underground provide a means for some of the traumas of war to be replayed.

The Tip, 1950s

The managers at the colliery do everything they can to leave detritus underground. They enforce low ceilings in narrow seams, pack worked-out roads with rubble, and reward mining teams who bring up high percentages of coal. But still the tip grows. Even for the proportions of Stoke-on-Trent, a city well versed in industrial giganticism from potbanks to steel mills, the conical shape of Chatterley-Whitfield's mountain is a landmark.

A conveyor belt on a gantry will run all the way to the top, depositing a stream of waste to form a cone to express the sizes, weights and shapes of everything discarded from the mine. Elsewhere though, the tip is an unmechanised throwback. Rails lead up an incline to finish at the edge, where trucks of dirt are tipped over. Much of the colliery is switching to electric winders now, and the bits that aren't rely on steam, but the incline is too steep for an engine and the tip-points too temporary for anything more complicated. Horses are still the solution. Long after the last pit pony exits the underground, building mountains of waste is one of the last operations to be animal-powered.

The horses bring out a side in the men not normally visible at the pit. On the one hand, they admire the sheer power horses have, and recognise their own bodies in the visible musculature as a mare strains under the load. On the other hand, the horses are pitied, and more so, it seems, because they represent the older conditions of the pit, before Acts of Parliament and nationalisation brought at least an attempt to make things safer for men. Or, perhaps it is the waste that is the problem here. A tip like this is not just waste from the mine—it is wasted labour to pit owners, wasted effort and bodies to labourers, and wasted lives for the horses.

But at least the tip itself isn't completely wasted. Away from the main dumping sites and out of view, children use the slope as a risky playground. They run up and down inclines, returning covered in coal dust, and worse. In the winter, the tip occasion-

ally works as a ski-slope, and at all times it offers a good view. Hardly an 'amenity' of the sort talked about in civic planning offices or amongst the designers of power stations, but used, at least. At other times, it is more impor- tant still. There is still coal here, and significant amounts of it if care is taken

to look. At times of need, coal-picking on this heap provides families with a means to heat their homes when other support disappears, and that despite the signs, so familiar in other contexts: "Trespassers will be Prosecuted".

The Barn Owl, 2017

There's a line of lenses outside the fence, as if a new football signing is just about to be unveiled. A fox ducks past, and a few briefly turn to catch it as it heads across the valley to Fegg Hayes foraging. Distraction over, the focus returns to a glass-less window high on the brick walls of the Winstanley heapstead

To be sure, the barn owl is the prize, but these cameras aren't just here for it. They aren't trained on the long grass, mice and voles of the country park, because the object here is to capture the creamy feathers of the owl against the dark angles of the colliery. The messaging is irresistible; nature 'taking back' an industrial ruin and the refuse of extraction; the rewilding of post-carbon economies. Yet this is not exactly right. The Barn Owl's heritage is the story of a species that spread around the world before us, but then took advantage of our farming, our landscapes. With the Barn Owl drifts our own lost ecology, and relationships between humans and wildlife that that the modern world has unravelled and never retied. Somewhere between the owl and the cameras, those heritages collide, mix, and produce images we find more comforting than we should.

Me, my partner and our unborn child sit half-way up the old tip, far enough away to observe both species, though we know from experience that nothing may ever happen. The owl is fickle, and is the expert on this site. It appears at the window, half-hidden, then, five minutes later, darts back into the window from the old railway sidings. We watch it reappear beyond the cameras, briefly quartering before diving into the grass. There's a certain comedy to watching frustrated photographers staring at a window with their backs to the owl, but they probably can't see it anyway. It's getting dark; some give up and wander off, when at last the owl consents and returns to the window right over their heads. The resultant scramble probably doesn't produce any decent shots, but at least their lenses got a glimpse.

We sit on top of one of the old mine cars for dinner. They are some of the last remnants of the museum—colliery name on the side, mock coal on the top, a useful ladder, offering the

mild peril of jumping between cars. We heat last nights' curry
on a stove, pausing to listen to rustlings in the grass around
us, and eat by moonlight and a security fence. The owl appears
at head height, travelling with a vole, or a mouse. It is not
the top bird here, and its flight even now isn't low enough. A
kestrel appears below it and upside down, talons grabbing the
catch. In this light, the bulk of feathers makes the challenge
appear foolhardy, but the kestrel is the acrobat, and the fight
has clearly happened before. The owl drops its prey in a second,
and we are left wondering if the kestrel lies in wait every time.

Matthew Kelly

The Line of the Pylons

All routes west of Southampton cross the River Test. Rising at Ashe, a tiny settlement in rural Hampshire near Overton, the Test flows through *Watership Down* country, before emptying into Southampton Water. Since the 1970s, when the M27 was cut through this Hampshire downland, connecting the port cities of Portsmouth and Southampton to the West, motorists doing seventy have had little cause to notice this celebrated chalk stream country. I know this, I've driven this way, oblivious to an indifferent ecology known for its flowering plants, invertebrates, and wetland birds. But I've also followed the Test Way and know from below of the concrete uncanny of the motorway flyover above.

Older ways telling of older modes of transport lie to the south. Redbridge Bridge crosses the Test at its lowest point. The current structure replaced a medieval crossing, and it's now a bridge of two halves, formed of adjoining seventeenth and eighteenth-century sections. Immediately south, the Redbridge Causeway carries the A36 east and west. Again, two structures. Westbound traffic took sole possession of the low-slung Redbridge viaduct, a fifty-year old concrete structure, when the adjacent concrete bridge was added, allowing two-lane traffic in both directions. Both shored up by recent structural work. The railway, dating from the 1840s, lies below on a raised bed, seemingly afloat on still waters.

Down river, the cranes of the Prince Charles Container Port crenelate the horizon. Cruise ships and ocean liners can be imagined anchored at Southampton Port beyond. The diesel generators powering idling ships, the continual flow of heavy lorries, and hypnotically long diesel-electric goods trains make Southampton one of Britain's most polluted cities. Heavy particulates lie low. From smaller ports, ferries carry commuters and trippers to the Isle of Wight and to Hythe, crossing the great rectangular river basin named Southampton Water that opens-up where the Test meets the Itchen. Broad passage and deep anchorage have long made Southampton Water a major commercial waterway. Its heavy flow is further supplied by the Hamble before it addresses The Solent, the busy seaway separating the Isle of Wight from the mainland.

The Redbridge bridges mark the southern boundary of the Lower Test Nature Reserve, where chalk stream wetlands provide habitat for wildflowers and overwintering wildfowl, but the bridges do not constitute an ecological boundary. Downstream on the Southampton side, river waters are marshalled by the heavily industrialised and urbanised east bank, but much of the Test's western shore is unbanked, the littoral changing with every tide. South-west from the bridges, against a mature forest backdrop, cattle graze low-lying land at the water's edge.

Despite the oscillating traffic racket, this distant tranquillity can evoke Dutch landscape painting. But this is no rustic idyll. Some decades ago, where the cows graze, the forest shore was cleared for industrial works and container yard. Shoreline trees diminish the visual impact of the works but not the containers, stacked orange, blue and red against the forest backdrop. They seem a joyful rather than an incongruous presence on a hot and bright day like today. The proximity of the railway to the containers and the flatbed lorries that carry them register two transport revolutions, both built to the scale established by nineteenth-century terrestrial transport infrastructure. The scale and promise of productive toil give this assemblage a picturesque quality.

This scaling is disrupted by the last component of this scene: the massive presence of twentieth-century energy infrastructure. Electricity pylons, planted two abreast at regular intervals, dominate the Test shoreline and partition the sky. Dense with strength and built to standardised design, these rangy steel structures sling across many miles the heavy cables that carry electricity north upcountry and across the Test to the city.

Today I've come to follow the line of the pylons to their sources, taking a way neither old nor new. The pylons link industrial developments that since the end of the Second World War have transformed these shoreline terrains from English pastoral

into something else. The first phase was celebrated by regional
boosters and a sympathetic press. It brought the huge Esso
oil refinery (1951), then Marchwood Power Station (1955),
International Synthetic Rubber (1958), Monsanto (1958), Union
Carbide (1960), Air Products (1961), Hythe Gasworks (1964),
and Fawley Power Station (1969), all built on agricultural land
acquired by Clement Attlee's Labour Government through a
compulsory purchase order. These interdependent anchor insti-

tutions instantiated the state-private petrochemical capital that underpinned post-war social democracy. 1,000s of jobs were brought to the region, driving the development of housing, roads, and amenities, creating a new peri-urban complex. Since then, village and agricultural life has co-existed with industrial workers, cul-de-sacs, supermarkets, and residential developments for the well-heeled attracted to the maritime environment.

As such, the littoral hosts a peculiar rural modernity, a hybrid landscape that somehow blends bucolic southern England with industrial modernity. This strip of shoreline, perhaps ten-miles by one-mile, is neither unspoilt countryside nor urban conurbation. Industrial and suburban but somehow more rural than urban, the littoral boasts neither centre nor ribbon development. Instead, an ersatz Hampshire—old pubs, working farms, pretty cottages, and pockets of obvious affluence—coexists with the oil refinery and the power stations and the chemical works and the new towns. Developments that elsewhere seem intrinsically or essentially North or Midlands are here made South.

Although an interest in emplacing post-war social democracy first drew me to Hampshire's rural modernity, I now have some inkling of how the region has since been shaped by intersecting processes of privatization and globalization. Today, as I follow the line of the pylons to their sources at Marchwood and Fawley, my route determined by footpaths and rights of way, I'll be alert to how energy infrastructure has shaped this landscape for several generations. Derelict sites will speak of deindustrialisation, redundancies, and the ghost presence of modernist buildings but I can hardly miss how financialised capital has seen much post-war industrial plant change hands several times, going through cycles of renewal and expansion as new investment has come this way. Change rather than decline tends to be the dominant story in affluent parts of the South, and aerial photographs from the 1960s indicate that the density of current building on the littoral—residential, industrial, and commercial—is greater than it has ever been. The most polluting industrial plant have gone or been cleaned up, and since the 1980s there has been some ecological restoration, but the concrete and tarmacadam footprint has advanced remorselessly. My purpose today is to grasp how this rurality was remade since the Second World War. Hence, dressed in shorts, t-shirt and sandals, a daysack on my back and a hefty camera tucked under one oxter, I'm standing on Redbridge contemplating pylons one very hot August morning.

Cutting down a path off the viaduct, past the haulage firm with the containers—large expanse of concrete—I'm soon in the village of Eling. Boats moored in the marina, kids splashing in shallows off the slipway, and a pound taken off motorists at the single-track toll bridge. I have coffee and toast in the café but pay little to attention to the 'Eling Tide Mill Experience', too buoyed by the walk ahead to be waylaid so early. From the far side of the bridge, The Anchor pub, recent apartments with south-facing balconies, and those colourful containers provide backdrop to the moored boats basking in the bright sunshine. Up past St Mary the Virgin, the tenth oldest church in England, and Homeway Cottages, whitewashed and reinforced with iron brackets, a pylon T-Junction directs wires from the South to the East and West. Fingerpost indicates that Marchwood is 2¼ miles and Fawley 9¾ miles distant. Trespassers are warned off at the entrance to Marchwood Aggregates.

The road is divided from a permissive footpath by a thick, brambly hedge of no great vintage. Blackberries ripen, dust clouds swirl in the brown-dry field. Another line of east-west pylons and the stumpy spire of Hythe village church in view. A small Southern Water treatment works in British brick municipal: state infrastructure, now privatised, prominently branded. Off the path, the wide sweeping road into Marchwood passes the Household Waste Recycling Centre and the deserted Marchwood Skate Park (sponsored by the Veolia Environmental Trust). Trees have shed their leaves against the assault from the summer's long heatwave.

Here the cranes, pylons, and containers that punctuate views of the shore are joined by the stocky twin chimneys of Marchwood Power Station. Smartly contemporary, the power station's all white and pleasingly simple shapes bespeak a minimalist architectural aesthetic. The original power station was completed on this site in 1955, planned by the Central Electricity Generating Board as a coal-fired power station but developed to burn fuel-oil at a late stage in its construction. On an adjacent site, the CEGB established the Marchwood Engineering Laboratories, one of its national research centres. Old photographs show modern industrial structures surrounded by fields. The research labs were run down and closed following privatization. Retired power workers lament the industry's failure to maintain the research and development capacity that characterised their careers in the industry and the public service remit of the CEGB. The area since developed into the private Marchwood Industrial Park.

In the village, by a small stretch of canal leading to the docks, a family paddles a rubber dingy in the lee of a moored ship and a couple of old boys fit a new propeller to a boat. We chat. They banter about the respective size of their pensions and how a woman must have lured me, obviously from the South, to the North East.

Can I take photos of the power station? *Just drive into the industrial estate and say you're going to the café if stopped by security. Won't be any trouble. Claim you're there on business.* I look down at my sandals.

At the entrance to the park, I'm immediately doubtful. Public access is not encouraged. Hailed by the security guard. Friendly, he buys the line about the café. I cannot take photographs without written permission. Company policy. Not the first time I'll hear this today. All very agreeable. Off I stroll. Not furtive at all. I quickly pass the sign for the café and enter the belly of the estate. Grab a picture of a transformer with the power station behind. Another one of the power station with an immediately adjacent pylon.

Electricity can seem an abstract force, the relationship between the plug in the wall and glowing laptop unfathomable to most of us. Today I'm struck by its materiality and basic simplicity. Marchwood Power Station burns gas to turn a generator which produces electricity which is fed directly into the grid through a big wire.

I'm not an activist trying to assert a right, just a historian wanting to see—and ideally photograph—a bit of infrastructure. I feel politely defiant when a security car slowly drives past and parks up ahead. I keep going. Casual posture. He drives on. It's a bit silly. At a quiet stretch of road, I get a lovely photograph of the power station from across a pond. Must be the one they use on publicity brochures.

Further on, the security car crawls past. The security guard is evidently no keener on a difficult conversation than I am. The road switches back. Magnificent view of the power station in full industrial splendour. I can't blatantly ignore the "no photography" instruction in the presence of the idling car. Surprised a little by my confidence, I approach the car and explain what I'm up to. The guard says he was radioed by the power station. It has shut the gates as a precautionary measure. They need to be careful, you see, what with the chemical plants, the power station, and the nearby military base. I get the message and take my leave, exiting to the south side of the industrial park. The road passes McMullen Barracks and the Sea Mounting Centre, where long trains of sealed railway carriages are drawn up in sidings. At the side of the road the scrub has been worn away where it is good to get a shot of the power station.

A can of full fat Coke in Marchwood Co-op is reviving. A bloke asks the shop assistant how much something is. Free if you take your top off, she cackles. Outside a Pole in a white van curses: "kurwa, kurwa, kurwa!" The First World War memorial recalls pre-industrial Marchwood: young farmworkers going off to war, some volunteers, some conscripts. Another memorial commemorates the men of the Royal Fleet Auxiliary killed during the Falklands Conflict. I cross the disused railway line formerly used to transport oil from the refinery to London and elsewhere. Now piped or barged. Built under the Light Railways Act 1896 and opened in 1925, passenger services were closed in 1966, freight in 2016. There's talk of reopening. Latterly British Rail Class 205 'Hampshire' diesel-electric units, assembled at nearby Eastleigh, carried human traffic. For me, the romance of the railways is diesel-electric: a generational thing. To this day, every major development proposed for the area raises objections about the absence of decent transport infrastructure.

I'm now following the A326 for a short stretch. Not much fun. Pass the entrance to a branch of the Priory Hospital. An oddly retro symbol of 1990s hedonism and its celebrity casualties.

On Veals Lane, I re-cross the railway line and find the footpath that will take me into Hythe. A care worker at a rest home fills my water-bottle but doesn't invite me to help myself to her tray of Calippos. Such is the power of suggestion, now the thing I want most in the world is a Calippo. Gate marking the entrance to the Right of Way hung with aggressive notices. Along the path high hedges sprout oaks that mask views of the salt marshes. So dry and crackling that underfoot it feels more Andalusia than Hampshire—lizards should scuttle in the under-growth—but the atmosphere is maritime.

The path is lined with trees, a bank rising on both sides. To the left as a tide-break and to the right is a mount for the railway, another industrial line carved through this agricultural landscape. A break in the hedge exposes the blocks of flats and tower at Woolston, brightly inscribed across Southampton Water. The flat littoral and calm waters have a foreshortening effect. Marchwood Power Station is clearly visible behind and a huge ARC tanker is moored in Southampton Water. Acorns fall onto the path at my feet. A dead hawk is half submerged in foliage on the verge.

Where Veals Farm threatened more surveillance than it probably delivered, Hythe Marina Village leaves the casual visitor sure they're watched. Cameras are everywhere and notices warn of guard dog patrols. Built in three phases beginning in 1985, each house comes with a mooring. Its denizens gather in The Boathouse to drink continental lager and large glasses of

Chardonnay. A period piece inspired by *Howard's Way*? Hythe proper boasts a more conventional foreshore and a main street that seems to pastiche a pretty village street, like that outlet shopping village in Oxfordshire. I follow the English Coast Path out of the village, scowling at its xenophobic banality, passing in quick succession a Waitrose, a red brick Victorian church, a Lidl, and some light industrial units. The headquarters of the 2495 (Hythe) Squadron of the Air Training Corps, the Hythe Sailing Club, and the Hythe Sea Scouts precede a stretch of salt marsh. Across Southampton Water the oil terminal at Hamble and the tower of the former military hospital at Netley peeps through the trees. Some form of topographical alchemy sees Shore Road becomes Frost Lane. I turn off onto Hart Hill and the footpath that will take me to the chemical works and the oil refinery.

The sandals weren't the best idea, not for a walk of this length. Not far from Hythe I'd become aware that a spot under the balls of both feet was rubbing. Two big blisters are forming. One or two little ones have ballooned between my toes. My feet are filthy. I fancy I've taken on an urchin-like quality or perhaps that of picaresque vagrant, but I probably most resemble a middle-aged man with dirty feet. 'Pressing on' has never felt so literal.

A low industrial hum is now pervasive, respecting neither the picture-book Traveller's Rest pub nor the small valley dense with mature forest behind. The source can be easily spied. Behind the pub car park and above the trees pokes the white stem and black stub of the Tredebe high temperature incinerator chimney. They'll take care of your hazardous organic waste. On an adjacent site are the GEO chemical works. The original plant was built by Union Carbide in the late 1950s, the company's second UK works after its first at Grangemouth in Scotland, another place where an oil refinery stimulated the development of petrochemical manufactures. At Union Carbide, Ethylene supplied by the Esso refinery was converted into ethylene oxide for multiple industrial uses. Beyond the Geo works is the former site of International Synthetic Rubber, established in 1956 by a consortium of rubber manufacturers led by Dunlop. As Britain's first venture—and Europe's second—into the bulk manufacture of synthetic rubber, it relied on butadiene extracted by the Esso refinery and styrene supplied by the Shell Chemical Company and Forth Chemicals. Not a serious challenge to US global dominance of the industry, but an attempt nonetheless to reduce the country's reliance on dollar imports. Later owned by Polimeri Europe UK, it was closed and then demolished in 2013, leaving behind a 54-acre brownfield site. None of this is visible from the path, which skirts the works, following a weaving, undulating way through woods, sunlight dappling the path. A clichéd description, but the path is clichéd pretty, the most clichéd pretty of the day. No need to get the thesaurus out. Still the hum. The works means no-one wants to build here. To my inexpert eye, the woodland thrives, but what effect has the constant drone had on birds and mammals? A clearing at the incinerator: grass dried light brown, green steel industrial fence, razor wire, CCTV, warehouses, chimney, warnings. Beyond the works, scrub has been sculpted into tracks for dirt bikes. Out there, somewhere, revs a lone two-stroke.

Planted in a verge, a concrete, paddle-shaped pipeline marker with the distinctive blue and red symbol of Esso tells of the industrial underworld. Its smooth facing surfaces and rough texture behind tell the haptics of childhood public spaces, 1970s and 80s municipal. The marker is inscribed with technical detail. If I'm reading it correctly, the pipe is fourteen inches in diameter and three kilometres from its source. A mix of imperial and metric.

A large white notice hangs on the gate to an outpost of the refinery. Remember the sinister notice signalling threat from the opening pages of *Watership Down*? This one describes the outcome of the case taken by Esso and Exxonmobile against Extinction Rebellion and the Just Stop Oil campaign in the High Court in early 2022. The judgement captures something of England's petrochemical geographies. It applies to the "Oil Refinery and Jetty at the Petrochemical Plant" at Fawley, the Hartland Park Logistics Hub in Farnborough, the Pumping Station at Holybourne in Hampshire, and the oil terminals at Hythe, Avonmouth, Birmingham, and Stanwell in Middlesex. Until April 2023, anyone trespassing, erecting structures, obstructing access, or "affixing any person or object" to these sites risks prison or the seizure of assets. Civil offences made criminal. Perhaps the encounter with the mild-mannered security guard at Marchwood had more to it then I realised. Rucksack, shorts, camera, stubble. I have the look of an XR activist. The hum, surveilled privatised space, and the threatening legal context gives new meaning to this walk. I came in search of the new landscapes of post-war social democracy, and I've found the basic infrastructure of fossil capital and the security state.

Here the refinery is low-rise red brick buildings, white and grey storage tanks, and exposed piping. Whereas everything was boxed inside clean-lined structures at Marchwood, this is a Bowellist tangle of pipes and tanks. The refinery, of which these structures are just the entrée, is Richard Rodger's Lloyd's Building and then some. At the private road to the Hythe Oil Terminal, the High Court judgement is again prominently displayed. A fingerpost gamely beckons me away and on along the England Coast Path.

Beyond the Lighthouse Community Church, the 'Path' becomes a long stretch of the A326, coursing with traffic skirting the refinery's long perimeters. The New Forest Academy urges 'Find your remarkable', but I make do with a Calippo from the Co-op at Holbury. Such are the state of my feet, I yowl with joy and relief as I pass the Welcome to Fawley sign. All Saints, Fawley in sharp contrast with the main entrance to the refinery a few steps on. I photograph the handsome red brick office block at the main entrance and immediately attract the attention of a security guard. He insists on watching me delete the picture. Company policy. I wonder about the legal status of this assertion of corporate power. The office building can be seen on Google Earth.

It's five o'clock, eight hours since I left Swaythling. The lane down to Ashlett Creek suffused with the balmy atmosphere of a summer's evening by the sea. Anchored at the Esso terminal is the Amundsen Spirit, a crude oil tanker, built in 2010. Named to honour the Norwegian polar explorer, it sails under the flag of the Bahamas, doubtless for tax purposes. Vesselfinder.com later says it was moored at Fawley for thirty-eight hours, having previously called at Stura, Norway. Next stop Rotterdam. A middle-aged woman in shorts walks her dog, following the gently sloping lane down to the shoreline.

Hereabouts the weathered faces of people who live in and around boats and the sea, signals a wholesome, happy life, evoking the peoples of Westcountry coastal landscapes I love so much. The tide mill, mill pond and pub at Ashlett Creek recalls Eling, but isolation has spared Ashlett Creek the suburbanising pressures that changed Eling. For the first time today, it feels like I've escaped not just the ambit of Southampton but also the tentacles of the congested, busy, and commercially pressured South East. It is truly peaceful. Folk idle away the evening in the sunshine. An act of will prevents me from popping into the Jolly Sailor (yes, really!) for a pint.

The tide is out, Ashlett's small floating piers and boats suckered into heavy mud. Morbid thoughts about my chances should I fall in. I shudder, press on, self-conscious about my blistered hobble.

Finally, I'm crossing Fawley's celebrated salt marches. Blues, browns, and greens burnished with a hint of gold by the evening sun. Sail boats fleck the water between here and Portsmouth's Spinnaker Tower, a giant plastic toothpick pointing into the sky. A new industrial hum. Fawley Power Station might not have generated electricity for a generation, but the transformer is still at work, introducing electricity carried by underwater cables from France to the National Grid. The Red Funnel ferry, sailing from the Isle of Wight to Southampton, sits high in the water. I think of Huck Finn.

Metal posts, mesh fencing, barbed wire and razor wire mark the boundary between the salt marsh and what was once Fawley Power Station, the final component of the industrial complex developed after the expansion of the oil refinery. When commissioned in the early 1960s, it epitomised oil-based industrial modernity and post-war optimism. Boasting a colossal output and an iconic chimney and control room, it heralded an energy rich future that promised industrial prosperity and a comfortable quality of life for all. Hubris. The oil shock meant electricity generated by oil-fired power stations dependent on oil imports quickly became horribly expensive. Thereafter, Fawley was fired up when there were shortages in the grid, enjoying the dubious distinction of having only worked at full capacity for an extended period during the miners' strike of 1985. EU environmental regulations sealed its fate, and it was closed in March 2013.

Now rebranded Fawley Waterside, the first I see of the site is a vast featureless warehouse, CCTV cameras and all-too-familiar warning signs about guard dogs and trespassers. In 2015, it was bought by a consortium led by Aldred Drummond, owner of the nearby Cadland Estate and son of Maldwin Drummond, who owned the site, like the rest of the nearby industrialised land, before it was acquisitioned by the Attlee government. A discarded sign, propped upside down against the inside of the fence, reads "NationalPower Private Property Keep Out". Give or take, the power station's forty-year operational life was divided equally between the public and the private sectors.

The site is not as deserted as it first seems. A well-looked after but unusual yellow coupé (a Mitsubishi?) is parked beside more ordinary cars. More warehouses, clean and smart. And, in front of the power station's famous control room, the last part of the original power station scheduled to be demolished, turbine propellors are stored, propped on stands, shockingly huge and shiny new. Giant ear trumpets. One energy regime slowly superseded by another.

I follow the path down the short southern side of the rectangular site. A Ukrainian flag whipped aloft by the breeze coming up from The Solent, symbolizes another energy shock. A look at the map indicates it's a longer back to the road than I thought. At the south-west corner of the site, fencing has been torn down and a rough path broken through the brush by the perimeter fence. It must be a locals' shortcut back to the road. For a few minutes the going is easy, but soon I'm pushing through scrub and brambles. The layer of mud and grit offers my bare shins little defence. Up ahead, on the other side of the fence, is temporary accommodation. A group of men sit outside, an itinerant workforce far from home. Unsure what to expect, I say hello and ask if I can get out this way. They're friendly, saying yes, gesturing ahead. I keep going, a bit sceptical. I greet a new group of workers. I feel a bit ridiculous, behind the fence, obviously where I shouldn't be. This lot are Geordies, eating Crunchies. Much banter, but I can't get a straight answer out of them about whether I can get to road this way. I do, though, find out who they are. This is the demolition team.

I ask if they did the chimney the previous September. *Oh yes. It was pissing down. Not that you'd know, drinking cappuccinos in the office.* And the Control Room? *You from the Daily Echo? Yeah, it'll go soon. Next few months. Want a Crunchie?* Can I get out here? *You got trainers on? You'll need to run, from the dogs. Nah, you'll be alright, if you can get over that fence. I'll just sit here, and watch you come running.* The supervisor, he who drank the cappuccinos, says he might be able to get security from the quarry to escort me out. The quarry...? *What, and tell them we've got a trespasser?*

Time to turn back. The long way around. I retrace my steps. The buses are running, but this late they don't come this far, just short of Calshot. I hobble the mile or two into Fawley village centre and take up my position in the bus shelter.

A bottle of Ribena delivers its sugar and Vitamin C shot. A closer look at my feet reveals a ginormous blister on my heel where the strap rubs. The serrated edge of a bitten nail is a useful tool. Little pool of bloody liquid expands on the pavement. Early in the bus journey back to Southampton some local kids smash an upstairs window. Once they're off at Holbury, the fuming 'drive' heads straight back to Southampton Central, skipping his stops. I take a taxi back to Swaythling.

Britain began refining oil in 1914. There were twenty-three refineries on the eve of the oil shock of 1973. By 2000, there were twelve, now there are seven. The brownfield sites of the petrochemical economy pepper Britain, archiving processes of expansion, concentration, and contraction, the consolidating efficiencies of industrial modernity. Most distinctive are the watermarks left in the landscape by the circular bases of demolished storage tanks. Like evidence of medieval field systems, these will fade with time, visible from the air to the discerning eye or on the ground during drought or snow. Landscape historians of the future will have to learn to see what we take for granted. To figure out the things that happened, they too might walk the Southampton Water littoral, navigating scarcely imaginable surveillance systems of future privatised space.

Katrina Navickas

....

Blackstone Edge

1. Ted Hughes, 'The Rock', in *Worlds: Seven Modern Poets* (Penguin, 1974), pp.124–25.
2. London Metropolitan Archives, 4287/02/252, Ramblers' Association files, 'Industrial Pennines', *Them's Our Hills*, September 1990.
3. M. Pollington, 'A New Survey of Blackstone Edge Road: Interim Results', *The Archaeological Forum Journal: CBA Yorkshire* (Volume 1) (2012), pp.53–58.
4. Edwin Waugh, *Snowed-up, or, the White House on the Moor Top* (Manchester, 1869), pp.11–15.
5. Keith Parry, *Trans Pennine Heritage: Hills, People and Transport* (Newton Abbot: David and Charles, 1981), pp.62–69.
6. J. B. Davenport, *Davenport's Hollingworth Lake Guide and Visitor's Handbook to Blackstone Edge, Littleborough and Milnrow* (Rochdale: E. Wrigley, 1861), pp.17–18.
7. Ernest Jones, 'Blackstone Edge', *Northern Star*, 22 August 1846.
8. Thanks to Gwyneth Morgan of East Lancashire Clarion Choir and the Blackstone Edge Gathering for sending me a copy of the 2019 songsheet. 'Fracking Anthem' lyrics by Simon Welsh, Balcome, 2013.
9. Taylor Parkes, 'The Fall and Mark E Smith As A Narrative Lyric Writer', *The Quietus*, July 2010, thequietus.com/articles/03925-the-fall-and-mark-e-smith-as-a-narrative-lyric-writer
10. Elain Harwood, 'Jerusalem to Prestwich', in Tessa Norton and Bob Stanley, eds., *Excavate! The Wonderful and Frightening World of The Fall* (Faber, 2021), p.17.
11. Justin Hopper, *The Old Weird Albion* (Penned in the Margins, 2017); Justin Hopper and Sharron Kraus, 'Bonny Breast Knot', *Chanctonbury Rings* LP (Ghost Box Records, 2019).
12. 'Plans refused for England's largest onshore wind farm on Scout Moor', 11 July 2017, *BBC News*, bbc.co.uk/news/uk-england-manchester-40532195
13. Nan Fairbrother, *New Lives, New Landscapes* (London: Architectural Press, 1970); Brenda Colvin, *Land and Landscape* (London: John Murray, 1948).
14. Sylvia Crowe, *The Landscape of Power* (London: Architectural Press, 1958).
15. As a side note, Matthew Kelly and I were among visitors given the opportunity to climb up to the base of the transmitter tower at Alexandra Palace, north London, in December 2018. We squeezed up to the roof through a hatch in the ceiling. It was among the most thrilling things I've ever done.
16. Guy Shrubsole, 'Who Owns England?' blog, 'Who Owns England's Grouse Moors?' whoownsengland.org/2016/10/28/who-owns-englands-grouse-moors/
17. *Manchester Evening News*, 18 April 2010.
18. Lancashire Archives, Lancashire CPRE annual report, 1950–1.

The moorland is always on the horizon. From Rochdale, especially. Rochdale spreads over the Roch valley, surrounded on three sides by the hills. You see the line of the landscape from anywhere you might stand. It's there, in the middle distance, not too close but not too far away. The line of hills changes with the weather, the time of day, the season. They're always there.

The moors are a presence in the back of your mind that you don't notice until you've left. Ted Hughes saw it too, from the other side of the Pennines. In 'The Rock', a semi-autobiographical piece for a 1974 Penguin collection, he wrote:

> You could not escape the moors. They did not impose themselves. They simply surrounded and waited. … And however rarely you climbed to investigate them in detail, they hung over you at all times. They were simply a part of everything you saw.[1]

In 1988, the Ramblers' Association included this section from Hughes's 'The Rock' in their pamphlet, *Them's Our Hills*, alongside extracts from Alfred Wainwright's *A Pennine Journey*, and J. B. Priestley's *The Good Companions*.

The Ramblers were campaigning against a suggestion from the government that large scale conifer planting could be part of a viable economic regeneration scheme. The Pennine moorland isn't naturally an evergreen forest site. It is deciduous where there are trees, bald or rocky where there aren't any, and in the sections set apart for grouse shooting, it is overwhelmingly heathery. The Department of Environment, as it was then, had previously accepted that conifer afforestation was unsuitable. But then the government did a u-turn, motivated by economic investment and a quick profit from forestry for timber. The Ramblers were particularly incensed that in a preparatory report about the proposals, the government had dubbed the region 'the Industrial Pennines'. The region was not a (de)industrial wasteland. The hills were an amenity for local residents and full of nature. The literature anthology sought to illustrate their cultural meaning.[2] The plan was dropped, though the impression that the region was post-industrial wasteland remained.

That's not to say that the southern Pennines aren't bleak. Blackstone Edge is among the bleakest parts of the range. An outcrop of millstone grit, Blackstone Edge is black stone. The highest point is about 1500 feet above sea level. Blackstone Edge physically divides Greater Manchester and Calderdale, or Lancashire and the West Riding of Yorkshire if you prefer. The medieval Aiggin Stone marks the boundary. The way-marking stone is where the Pennine Way crosses. When the clouds are intermittent, the Edge is dark then light in succession, shadowed from the sun and then uplit in the beams again. You can see it from many vantage points in Rochdale: from the platform of the railway station, from the top of Halifax Road, from Cronkey Shaw Common. It is simply a part of everything you see.

Manchester Times, 30 March 1894

To climb to the Edge from Littleborough, you can just follow the main road, the A58. Most walkers prefer to turn off the road and go through Lydgate, and then climb the Roman Road. It isn't really a Roman Road. It follows the rough route of the main Roman Road that linked York to Chester, but the stones aren't that old. Archaeological investigations have dated them to 1725, when a turnpike was constructed.[3] The stones were laid to facilitate the transport of woollen cloth over the tops, the region's first industrial textile output before cotton. The road is about sixteen feet wide, with a central channel between the stones. The channel may once have accommodated a cable that was used to winch vehicles up the incline. It is likely that the stones were laid over an older packhorse route. This is a place that has always experienced human activity.

The White House is at the top, a pub that dates from the packhorse days. White against black. It sits alone in the moorland, a site of welcome for walkers, but also a site of deviance, of secret trysts and illicit dealings. Local dialect writer Edwin Waugh published a short story, 'Snowed-up (or, the White House on the Moor Top)' in 1869. In the introduction, reflecting on fifty years previously, he described the pub as a "welcome resting place", frequented by "curious company—company marked with characteristics which have now entirely disappeared". I'm not entirely sure what characteristics he meant. Waugh's loyalties to Lancashire were deep. He noted it was the last building of any kind when leaving the land of the red rose, and the first to greet weary walkers who had made the seven mile ascent from Sowerby Bridge and the West Yorkshire villages.[4]

Victorian antiquarians became obsessed with the Roman Road. Completely obsessed with it. The Victorians looked two ways: they were modern, and they were antiquarian. They had steam trains and gas lighting. Not soon later they had electricity. But they looked to the distant past too. Historic and archaeological societies abounded. Antiquarians sought to prove that anything old looking had its origins in the Roman settlement, or pagans, or Druids, or anything. As long as it was older than the modern age.

The turnpike was modern in its age. Turning off the road, you cross over concrete drainage channels, cutting through the slopes. These channels connect Blackstone Edge Reservoir, Green Withens Reservoir, and all the gathering grounds forming a vast network of water distribution. Pylons. The power lines slice over your head as you ascend the old road. And what can you hear? Wind, yes, but also the constant rumble of cars. The M62 slices across the landscape. Concrete, majestic, the Rakewood viaduct cuts across a dip. The road is held up by a series of four concrete pillars. The pillars repeat four upon four upon four, like gates or styles, but on a massive scale.

The 2014 Tour de France held its first couple of stages in Yorkshire. I went to watch the Grand Depart sweep through the moorland at Blackstone Edge. It was warm, and sunny, and large clouds drifted over the crowds. It felt as if the whole

of Littleborough village had climbed the Roman Road. We lined the road. This was a festival, albeit a very linear one (above). The route of the Tour passed through a few hundred yards on the boundary, in the old county. We stood in that bit, of course. I carried a Lancashire flag, yellow with the red rose, somewhat ironically. Others had a "welcome to Lancashire" sign.

It was a long morning of waiting until the caravans of sponsored goods sped past, throwing free samples out at the crowd followed by the inevitable bun fight to grab them. Then the cyclists came up Cragg Vale, and whizzed along the A58, their bodies blurred. And then they were gone. And we all tramped back down the Roman Road.

On a clear day, the view stretches to Manchester across the valley. Looking the other way along the tops, Stoodley Pike, the next landmark on the ridge boundary, is easily visible. Down below, is the calm water of Hollingworth Lake.

Hollingworth Lake is an artificial reservoir. It has a distinctive shape, like a claw or a shrimp, easy to identify on a map or on Google Earth. It was constructed by the engineer William Jessop in 1797 for the Rochdale Canal, which opened in 1804. From the lake, water was pumped up into a feeder channel at 600 feet that stretched for four miles along the valley side before discharging into the higher reservoirs. Oldham and Rochdale Corporations bought the lake in 1923 along with other Rochdale Canal Company reservoirs for their water supply. The maintenance track alongside the feeder linking Blackstone Edge (below) to Light Hazzles reservoir became part of the Pennine Way national trail in 1965.[5]

Almost from its opening, Hollingworth Lake became a pleasure ground. It quickly became a site for boating, birdwatching, fish-and-chips, and amusements. It was a destination for Victorian holidaymakers and textile workers on their day off. It still is today. J. B. Davenport's *Hollingworth Lake Guide and Visitor's Handbook to Blackstone Edge* in 1861 promoted its attractions. The guide pointed to the proliferation of photographers' studios and galleries, the new technology of the age. In a rather paternalist tone, Davenport also tried to regulate visitors' behaviour. He complained that the thousands of the Lancastrian working class were unfamiliar with the ways of a boat or the flora and fauna of the countryside, and that they should learn to respect the pleasures of nature.[6]

It takes about an hour to circumnavigate the lake. Or rather, to promenade it. Just enough for a Boxing Day forced march with the fractious family. From there, you either go and have candy floss or chips from the lakeside shops. School parties and scout groups undertake outdoor education, getting kitted out in ill-fitting lifejackets and turning themselves over in plastic kayaks. What I always stopped to look at on the way round was the overflow, its concrete dam waiting for its day to do the job it was built for.

If the day's fine, and you're bored of the amusements, what is there to do but take the hike up the Roman Road. I've walked up there when it was raining. Your feet slip against the stones. You get near the top and the cloud cover prevents you seeing much. And you go back down, hoping not to fall down. You can see as far as Manchester, number one Deansgate glinting against the sun. You can carry on to Stoodley Pike and Todmorden, following the Pennine Way.

Chartists held their mass meetings up Blackstone Edge in the 1840s. There's a natural amphitheatre in a dip in the hills near the stones. The Chartists spotted its potential for amplifying the voices of the speakers and the singers. Blackstone Edge became a symbolic spot, of freedom and liberty of working people against the oppression of the factory masters in the towns down below. From this vantage point they could look down on their masters. From this vantage point they could breathe clean(er) air, and escape the dirt and dust of industrial life. The Chartists walked up to the Edge from both sides, Lancashire and the West Riding. It was a cross-Pennine meeting point. Ernest Jones, perhaps the Chartists' best poet, composed a hymn for the mass meeting in 1846:

> But waved the wind on Blackstone height
> A standard of the broad sunlight,
> And sung, that morn, with trumpet might,
> A sounding song of Liberty. [7]

There's an annual commemoration of the Chartists meeting up Blackstone Edge (opposite, Chartist Gathering, 2017). Attendance varies depending on the weather. Sometimes us historians go up in a group. Usually the rest of the assembled are the usuals: the regulars who commemorate the Peterloo Massacre in Manchester as well, socialists of various stripes and trade unionists, mostly from the Lancashire side but a few brave souls come up to the tops from the Yorkshire side from Todmorden and Ripponden.

Sheltering beneath the edge, the East Lancashire Clarion choir lead the songs. As at many left-leaning commemorations, some songs are favourites: the Internationale, as always, some Billy Bragg tunes. Other songs are chosen to stay true to the commemoration: Jones's hymn gets an airing, sung from a sheet as no-one really remembers the lyrics by heart. And further songs are familiar tunes fit to new words. Saving the NHS, and defending the Lancashire plains against fracking for gas. So the 'Fracking Anthem' by Simon Welsh gets an airing: "And did they frack in ancient times? / Poisoning water once so clean?"[8] The gathering epitomises the eclecticism of the English radical tradition, mixing traditional patriotic tropes with historicism, commemoration and new political issues. Not everyone agrees with each other. But we all love the view from the top.

The choir's anti-fracking song is sung to the tune of 'Jerusalem'. 'Jerusalem' is not patriotic. Nor does it now refer to the English landscape that radicals or mystics see. This view from Blackstone Edge used to look over the "dark satanic mills" from above—if we take the meaning of mills to be chimneys. The government, in their afforestation plans in 1988, dubbed the Pennines "dark satanic hills". The Ramblers' Association complained about that term too. They disagreed that these moors were post-industrial wastelands. The landscape was an amenity for local residents.

Now the landscape is a site of regeneration schemes, private housing estates of cut-and-paste houses, Victorian warehouses converted into luxury flats while modern warehouses are clad boxes of distribution centres. A sea of buildings making up the neo-liberal economy. This is England. This is the North.

"The North will rise again." *The N.W.R.A.*

The Clarion Choir don't sing that one. Mark E. Smith applied a Lovecraftian stream of consciousness combined with the mysticism of Arthur Machen to the sound of Captain Beefheart in his lyrics. He lifted excerpts from William Blake too.[9] The Fall are usually associated with a highly urban setting, the back-street boozers of Prestwich and the crumbling Victorian central Manchester in the 1970s and 1980s. *The N.W.R.A.* envisages the Arndale shopping centre razed by the rebellion. But, as Elain Harwood points out in her essay on the landscapes of The Fall, the hills were still there in the background.[10] They were simply a part of everything Smith saw.

The landscape remembers. Justin Hopper, writing about the South Downs in East Sussex, stressed how landscape remembers. He was looking for Roman, Druid and prehistoric traces, the marks of shepherds and witches on the gentle chalk slopes. The grooves echoing every footfall and wheelroll, "like lines written on a face".[11] The Roman Road at Blackstone Edge perhaps no longer remembers its original creators. The millstone grit is hard, cut deep by the Ice Age. Not like the chalk of the Downs. Paths trodden by Chartists, Jacobites, Roundheads, the Pilgrimage of Grace, chapters of English protest history now only commemorated by re-enactors. The N.W.R.A.

The Pennine landscape has always been a source of energy production. Water, to power the canals and the cotton mills, initially. Electricity, to power the twentieth century. Landscape architect Sylvia Crowe depicted the mid-century British countryside as a "landscape of power". The Pennines have power.

The Super Grid line of pylons was constructed here in the 1950s. The upgrade to the National Grid, which had been built before the War, was challenged by local conservationists and countryside preservationists. The new pylons carried 275 kW, and were 136 feet high. The wind farms have faced major public opposition too. You can see the turbines turning over Scout Moor from here. Peel Energy sought to extend the existing wind farm by sixteen turbines of 115 metres high. Planning permission had been approved, but following a public inquiry by Rochdale and Rossendale councils in 2016, the government rejected the proposals for fourteen turbines in Rossendale, but approved the plans for two in Rochdale.[12] Fracking is now the key point of conflict, though it takes places on the plains and estuaries rather than the uplands.

Crowe was a key shaper of ideas on rural planning and infrastructure, alongside her compatriots Nan Fairbrother and Brenda Colvin. Their books on landscape now form a holy trinity of rural modernism.[13] Or at least their books look good together on those Ladderax shelves in one's Span designed flat, non? Mid-century modern is big concrete dams and the cooling towers of power stations as much as it is Danish teak sideboards or Festival of Britain pattern curtains.

Scale was the most important thing for these landscape architects. As long as the pylons, the transmitters, the motorways, were grand in scale, monumental, Crowe believed, then they were in context. They fitted the scale of the moorland. The transparency of the design was also crucial. She praised the open steel frames of the pylon: "It is this almost airborne quality which makes them far less obtrusive than a solid structure, despite their height, provided clean lines and simplicity maintain their grille-like character."[14]

The moors are also landscapes of communication. Radio and TV transmitters are ideally sited on moorland. They need the height, and the lack of trees, and the lack of population. Winter Hill transmitter near Bolton in the western spur of the Pennines. Travelling up the M6, you knew you were near home when you could see Winter Hill. TV transmitters are beacons, drawing our mental regional boundaries. Yes, we are still in Granada region here, even though it is long gone.[15]

The moors are commons, though technically they are manorial wastes, non-cultivated ground originally belonging to a manor. Blackstone Edge is common land, by virtue of section 193 of the Law of Property Act 1925. The legislation gave the public the right of access "for air and exercise" on all commons and wastes within borough or urban district council boundaries. Blackstone Edge might seem far from urban, but it was within the bounds of Littleborough Urban District Council, as it was.

But the right to roam is always limited. It's limited by the four Gs: gathering grounds, golf, grouse, and guns.

Gathering grounds. The water companies never liked public access to the gathering grounds of the reservoirs. At some reservoirs in other parts of the Pennines—at Winter Hill near Bolton, and at Bingley moor in West Yorkshire, campaigners organised mass trespasses from the 1890s to the 1930s. The trespasses might not have had such canonical status in the right to roam movement as the 1932 Kinder Scout Mass Trespass, although the 1896 Winter Hill trespass is now being commemorated. The trespasses nevertheless were demonstrations of the attachment locals had to the Pennine landscape. People walked. They hiked. However polluted or industrial this landscape became, it was a site of recreation. Water companies could not stop them.

Golf. Whittaker golf club was established in 1906. It sits alongside the Blackstone Edge Old Road. The fairways are lush green grass rather than scrub, striped by the mower. The hedges are silver birch, delineating each hole. Another form of enclosure, but for leisure rather for sheep, as the drystone walls further up the hill also enclose.

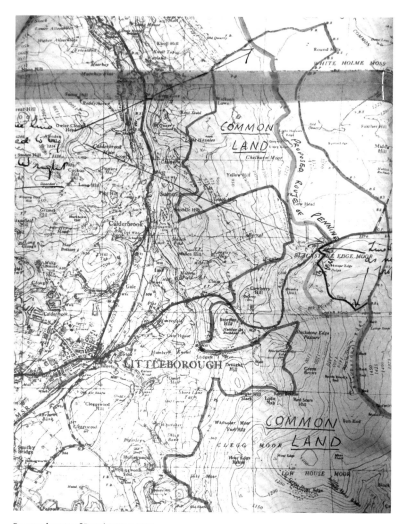

Proposed route of Pennine Way, 1951

Grouse. The landscape of Pennine moorland is heathery because of grouse shooting. In the mid nineteenth century, grouse shooting became increasingly popular among the gentry and wealthy manufacturers who emulated them. It also changed form. No longer did hunters need to follow grouse on foot. They waited behind newly constructed grouse butts, and sent their dogs out to drive the birds towards them. There are no grouse moors in the immediate vicinity of Blackstone Edge, but further south, around Saddleworth moor, the heather burns on the estates. Land campaigners point to the environmental, ecological and social impact of the 150 grouse moor estates in England.[16] The dull thud of the shot in the distance when you're out walking in the Peak District is ever present. With the firing of guns comes the firing of heather. Almost every summer in the 2010s, wildfires swept across the southern Pennines. The fires from Ripponden fanned by wind towards Blackstone Edge were probably begun by gas from the peatbogs.[17] The fires around Bolton and Stalybridge were grouse habitat management that got out of control.

Guns. Military requisition of vast swathes of moorland across the country also restricted the right to roam. In 1946, the armed services controlled nearly a million acres of land in England, but were calling for the acquisition of a further three million acres. Blackstone Edge was among the sites mooted by the Ministry of Defence for a South Lancashire Training Area. The others were near Anglezarke reservoir in the western spur of the Pennines near Bolton, and at Hailstorm Hill in the Rossendale Valley. Blackstone Edge was saved because of its proximity to the leisure facilities at Hollingworth Lake, and because conservationists worried that the tank manoeuvres might damage the Roman Road.[18] Anglezarke was chosen. The scars remain.

Moorland changes uses, landownership, amenity value, designations, modernity. The transmitters, the pylons, the wind turbines, will be replaced by something else in the near future. But the moors are always there. It is everything you see.

Opposite: "Blackstone Edge Moor. One of the sites proposed for a South Lancashire Training Area. View from mortar range on Clegg Moor across Blackstone Edge Road towards Chelburn Reservoir." Lancashire CPRE annual report, 1949.

Ian Waites

Observations relative chiefly to Picturesque Beauty and the West Burton Power Station

"An illustration of that beautiful species of landscape, produced by an *extensive vale*. Gradation is among the first principles of picturesque beauty. A graduating light, a graduation shade, or a graduating distance, are all beautiful... it is pleasing to see it fading away gradually, from the fore-ground, into the obscurity of distance."

"An illustration of that kind of *flat country…* The horizon is generally bounded by a distance, and yet seldom an extensive one; as there is rarely a rising ground, that can command it. The country is uninteresting, and wants adventitious objects to set it off."

"But with *three*, you are almost sure of a good group, except indeed they all stand in the same attitude, and at equal distances. They generally however combine the most beautifully, when two are *united*, and the third a little *removed*. *Four* introduce a new difficulty in grouping. *Separate* they would have a bad effect. The only way, in which they will group well, is to *unite three...* and to *remove the fourth*."

"Nature is always great in design… but she is seldom so correct in composition, as to produce a harmonious whole… something or other is not exactly what it should be."

"…that disposition of objects, which, by a partial and uncertain concealment, excites and nourishes curiosity."

"The two principal defects in the composition of landscape, that of objects being too crowded or too scattered."

"It is true, that a rich man, to whom the whole belonged, might pull them down, and place in their room a tower, a temple, or some ornamental building; but, besides that there is something unpleasant in destroying for the sake of mere ornament the marks of industry and habitation…"

Quotations

p.71 / p.72 / p.79
William Gilpin, *Observations relative chiefly to Picturesque Beauty, Made in the Year 1772, on Several Parts of England; particularly the Mountains, and Lakes of Cumberland and Westmorland*, vol.I, 1786.

p.80
William Gilpin, *Observations on the River Wye and several parts of Wales, etc., relative chiefly to Picturesque Beauty*, 1782.

p.87 / p.88
Uvedale Price, *Essays on the Picturesque, as compared with the Sublime and the Beautiful*, 1810.   .

p.95
Sir Uvedale Price, 'On Architecture and Buildings &c', in *Sir Uvedale Price on the Picturesque: with an essay on the origin of taste, and much original matter, by Sir T. D. Lauder, Bart*, 1842.

Image acknowledgements

Copyright Coal Authority. All rights reserved 2022: p.13, pp.14–15, p.18, p.19, p.20, pp.25–26, p.27, pp.28–29. Royal Commission on the Historical Monuments of England (RCHME) Archive Collection, Historic England: p.16. Andrew Mason Photography: p.31. Kelcey Swain, Creative Commons: p.24. Lancashire Archives, Lancashire Council for the Preservation of Rural England: p.63, pp.65–67.

Unless otherwise specified, image copyright lies with the author of the piece in which it appears.

Biographies

Ben Anderson is an environmental historian from Keele University, with an interest in the material relationships between people and landscape. He has worked on mountaineering and hill-walking in turn-of-the-century Europe, as well as on the 'decommissioned' infrastructures and their communities discussed here, histories of ultraviolet light in the late twentieth century, and the potential of creative methods to inform future historical research.

Matthew Kelly is an Environmental Historian at Northumbria University. He is interested in how rural environments in modern Britain and Ireland became sites of conflict in the face of developmental pressures, agricultural as well as industrial, and how these conflicts were shaped by new notions of environmental justice and citizenship. His latest book was published in paperback in 2023. It looks at four women environmentalists and has a slightly hyperbolic title: *The Women Who Saved the English Countryside* (Yale, 2022).

Katrina Navickas is a historian of politics, protest and landscapes. Originally from Rochdale, she now lives in Croydon. Outside her academic research, she has published guides to Croydon architecture and planning for Open City London and for the 20th Century Society. She formed the Rural Modernism network alongside the other contributors to this book.

Ian Waites is a historian of post-WW2 English society and culture, with particular interests in post-war planning, landscape, pop music. He is currently obsessed with the relationship between railway bridges and English country lanes. More productively, he has recently been helping a friend to write up his memoirs of being a teenage activist for the Committee of 100 (the direct action arm of CND) during the early 1960s, and is planning to publish a short guide to Radburn layouts on 1960s and '70s English housing estates.

We would like to extend our warmest thanks to Prof. Ceri Morgan for offering feedback on all our pieces.